Flower Power

Ann Walsh

Orca currents

ORCA BOOK PUBLISHERS

Library and Archives Canada Cataloguing in Publication

Walsh, Ann, 1942-
Flower power / Ann Walsh.
(Orca currents)

ISBN 10: 1-55143-386-9 / ISBN 13: 978-1-55143-386-8

I. Title. II. Series.
PS8595.A585F56 2005   JC813'.54   C2005-904076-9

First published in the United States, 2005
Library of Congress Control Number: 2005929720

Summary: Callie's mother has chained herself to a tree.

Mixed Sources
Cert no. SW-COC-001271
© 1996 FSC
FSC

*Orca Book Publishers is dedicated to preserving the environment and has
printed this book on paper certified by the Forest Stewardship Council.*

Orca Book Publishers gratefully acknowledges the support for its publishing
programs provided by the following agencies: the Government of Canada
through the Canada Book Fund and the Canada Council for the Arts,
and the Province of British Columbia through the BC Arts Council
and the Book Publishing Tax Credit.

Cover photography by Acclaim Images

ORCA BOOK PUBLISHERS
PO Box 5626, Stn. B
Victoria, BC Canada
V8R 6S4

ORCA BOOK PUBLISHERS
PO Box 468
Custer, WA USA
98240-0468

www.orcabook.com
Printed and bound in Canada.

13 12 11 10 • 6 5 4 3

Chapter One

It was early Saturday morning and something was scratching against my bedroom window. *Scritch. Scritchy-scratch.* I knew that sound. It was the branches of the maple tree. They tapped on my window when the wind blew. It was too early to get up, so I ignored the scratching. I was almost asleep again when the maple tree spoke, "Callie Powers. Wake up."

Never in the twelve years that I'd slept in this bedroom, never in my whole life had the maple tree talked. It often reached over and tapped on my window, but I had never heard it talk. Not until now.

I slipped out of bed and went to the window to take a closer look.

Mom was perched on a branch of the tree, right outside my window. I blinked and looked again. Mom waved. I blinked once more and rubbed my eyes. She was still there. The June sun was already up, and I could see her clearly as she reached out to poke at my window with the bristly end of a broom.

"Dream," I said to myself and turned around to go back to bed. "This has got to be a dream."

"Callie, come here," called Mom, and she rapped hard against the window-pane with the stick end of the broom. "Right now!"

That was not a voice Mom uses in my dreams. It was the voice she uses when she wants something done immediately. I was not dreaming. Neither was Mom. But she *was* sitting in a tree, and even for my mother that's unusual.

"What are you doing?" I asked, sliding the window open and yawning at the same time. "Why are you in the tree? Why is that chain around your ankle?"

"I need your help, Callie. Go downstairs. Beside the phone is a list of places I want you to call."

"Before breakfast?"

"Before anything. Start phoning."

"But it's too early. No one will be up yet."

"You'll be calling offices. Newspapers. TV stations. They'll have answering machines or voice mail. Read what I wrote for you to say—every word, Callie—and make sure you give our address."

3

"But Mom, you promised to take me shopping for jeans this morning."

"Your new jeans will have to wait. This is important."

"But, Mom…," I began again.

"Just do it, Calendula."

She was using her "or else" tone of voice. She also used my full name, another danger sign. The last time I argued with her when she was in that kind of mood, I found myself grounded for a week.

I didn't even brush my teeth or grab a glass of juice before I began phoning. The first call was the hardest because I got a real newspaper reporter, not the answering machine I had hoped for.

"*Westside Tribune*, Peter speaking."

"Hello, my name is Callie Powers and my mom is up a tree."

"Don't you mean your cat is up a tree, kid?"

"No, my mom."

"Try the fire department. They're good at getting cats out of trees. Maybe they also rescue mothers."

"You don't understand," I said. "I'll read what Mom wrote down."

"Okay, I've got a minute. Go for it."

I read, "I, Dianthus Powers…"

"Dianthus? What kind of name is 'Dianthus'?"

"It's a flower, like a small carnation. Why don't you just call her Dian? Everyone does."

"Dianthus is fine. How do you spell it?"

I spelled it for him, then went on reading Mom's press release. "I, Dianthus Powers, have chained myself to my neighbor's maple tree and will stay here until he agrees to leave it standing. I will be holding a press conference at the tree at ten o'clock this morning. Please attend."

"Your Mom wrote that?"

"Of course she did," I snapped. "I'm not up the tree, am I?"

"She sounds like an interesting lady," he said.

"That's not exactly the word I'd use to describe Mom."

He chuckled. "I know what you mean."

"How could you? Do you know my mom?"

"No. But…"

"Look, I've got a lot of calls to make. Are you coming to the press conference or not?"

"I wouldn't miss it for the world. But what do you think about what your mom is doing, kid?"

"Think? I think this is the craziest thing she's ever done, and she's done some really weird stuff. And don't call me 'kid,' please. I'm twelve."

He laughed. "I look forward to meeting you—and your mom," he said. "I'll be there. Count on it."

I put a check mark on Mom's list beside the name of his paper, *Westside Tribune*. "Okay," I said. "Here's our address."

"See you soon," he said and hung up.

Twenty calls later, I put down the phone, grabbed some juice and went upstairs to talk to Mom. She had disappeared, but I knew she was still there. The long chain that was locked around a branch snaked into the door of the tree house.

I pushed the window open as far as it would go. "Mom? I called everyone on the list. I'm going to get breakfast now."

The chain rattled, then the broom popped through the door, followed by Mom's head. She had bits of cobwebs and maple leaves stuck in her hair and a smudge of dust on her cheek. It must be cramped for her in there, I thought. It was a great tree house with glass windows and a real door, but it wasn't very big. Even I could barely stand up in it anymore. It was dirty too, because I hadn't kicked out the spiders since last summer.

"Good idea," Mom said. "I'll have tea and toast."

"You want breakfast too?"

"I'm protesting, Calendula. I am not on a hunger strike," she said, tossing the wicker basket at me. It slid along a wire stretched between the tree and a hook above my window. Mom had put the wire up a long time ago. She'd sent me a lot of peanut butter sandwiches and lemonade in that basket over the years.

"Make me a thermos of tea, Callie. Put blackberry jelly, the calorie-reduced stuff, on my toast. Four slices, please."

Mom pulled her head back into the tree house and I heard the broom swishing away, the end of it banging on the ceiling. Except for the noise and the chain sticking out of the door, you'd never have known she was tucked away in my tree house. Not unless you were the one who had to bring her breakfast. And lunch too, I thought. And dinner.

She had promised to take me shopping today, I thought. She had promised! I should be heading to the mall, not to the kitchen. When was I supposed to find time to do my homework if I had to do all this cooking and phoning?

I sighed and reached for the basket. Maybe Mom would come down by lunchtime, I thought. Maybe.

How long did she plan on protesting, anyway? How long was my mother going to live in a tree?

Chapter Two

While I made Mom's toast and filled
the kettle, things started to make sense.
Not that anything Mom did made much
sense. That's one of the reasons she
and Dad split up. Mom says that Dad
didn't understand her creative nature.
She also says that Dad is a boor who'd
rather watch pro wrestling than read
a book. I don't remember much about

the divorce, and I don't remember Dad ever watching wrestling. He does watch football and hockey. Sometimes I really miss him. Watching a hockey game with Mom isn't the same. She doesn't know the names of the players or the teams or anything.

I figured that Mom was in the tree because of the fight she'd had with Harold Wilson the night before. He's our next-door neighbor, and the maple tree grows on his side of the fence. His family bought the house next door years ago, about the same time my grandparents moved into this house.

I had been on my way to the kitchen to make popcorn when I heard their voices in the living room. Both Mom and Mr. Wilson sounded upset. I forgot about the popcorn and stayed in the hall to listen.

"It's time that tree went, Dian," he told her. "The tree house too. Callie hasn't used it in months. Why should I let it take up so much of my yard? For the sake of old times?"

"How can you even think of getting rid of the maple, Harold? Or the tree house? Your father helped build it."

Mom had told me that when they were young, she and Mr. Wilson and their friends spent a lot of time in the tree house. They stayed out until the night became too dark and they got scared. I used to do that too, but not this year. Most of my friends aren't into tree houses anymore.

Neither am I.

I wondered if Mom had been remembering the things she used to do when she was a kid and that's why she got so mad at Mr. Wilson.

"The tree house is probably half rotten," he said. "If a kid falls from it, I could be sued. Besides, I need a garage and that's the only place I can put one. So the tree has to go."

"Why do you suddenly need a garage?"

I peeked into the living room then, and I saw him blush. "For my bike," he said, not looking at Mom. "My Harley."

"A bike? That monstrosity parked outside is yours?" Then Mom laughed. "But you're an accountant. You don't even know how to ride a motorbike."

"I do too," he said. "I joined a club. I'm learning to…"

"A motorcycle gang? You belong to a *gang*?"

"No. It's a club. It's not a gang."

"A club?" Mom laughed again. "A club for aging accountants trying to regain their youth?" she asked. "It won't work, you know. You'll still go bald."

"I'll have you know that I ride very well, Dian. I'm even learning to repair the bike myself. I need a garage so I can work on it and lock it up at night."

Mom got angry. "So in your fight against middle age, you will destroy anything from your real childhood, right? Memories and heritage and neighborhood values—don't these things mean anything to you?"

"No," he said, and stood up. "Not anymore. The tree's coming down the day after tomorrow. I'll clean up any branches that fall on your side of the fence."

He stalked out, slamming our front door.

"Did you hear that, Callie?" Mom called. "Don't bother answering. I know you were listening." She thumped downstairs to her studio. I was glad when I heard the potter's wheel begin to hum. When she was angry or stressed, Mom felt better after she worked on her pottery. Besides, if she was busy in the basement then she wasn't upstairs getting mad at me.

I was kind of mad at Mr. Wilson myself. Sure, I didn't use the tree house much anymore, but that didn't mean I wanted it gone. During a hot summer, the tree house was a good place to be with a book and a can of cold pop. It always felt cool out there, and it was quiet and peaceful with the leaves waving all around you.

I'd wondered if I should write a letter to Mr. Wilson, asking him to leave the tree alone, but I didn't know what to say after "Dear Mr. Wilson."

I'd thought Mom could help me write the letter. She's good with words.

But I didn't have a chance to ask her. She hadn't come up from the basement by the time I went to bed. And this morning she was chained to a tree.

Chapter Three

I had just swung Mom's breakfast out to her in the basket when the doorbell rang. "Got to go," I said before she noticed that her toast was cold and that I'd put real sugar instead of sugar substitute in her tea. "Someone's at the door."

The someone turned out to be a skinny guy with thick glasses and a notebook. "Peter Dawl from the

Westside Tribune," he said. "I spoke to you, remember?"

"Your name is Peter Doll? Really?"

"Not 'doll,' Dawl. D-A-W-L."

"It sounds the same to me."

"It does to everyone. Unfortunately."

"Good thing you're not a girl and your parents decided to call you Barbie," I said.

"My mom did want to name me Ken."

"My mom wanted to name me— never mind," I said.

"So, where is your mom? Where's this tree?"

"Around the side of the house," I told him. "You can't miss them."

"She's really up in a tree?"

"Go see for yourself."

"Some people's mothers," he said, shaking his head. "Some people's mothers are weird."

"Well, mine is anyway," I said.

17

"But not all the time. Sometimes she's just like everyone else's mom."

Peter Dawl grinned. "What's your name, kid? Sorry. I'm not supposed to call you kid, am I?" His glasses moved up and down his nose as he spoke and I realized he reminded me of Clark Kent. Superman, when he's being a wimp instead of a hero. But this guy's black hair wasn't slicked down like Clark Kent's. It stood up in little wisps on top of his head. I was sure he hadn't used hair gel to style it that way.

"Callie," I said. "Don't ask me what it's short for."

"Okay, Callie, how do you feel about your mother's political stand?" He pulled a pencil from behind his ear. Then he dropped his notebook. I waited for him to get organized.

"Mom's not standing," I said. "She's hunched down inside a tree house. Talk to her, not me."

I shut the door in his face and ran to answer the phone. "Is this the Powers home? Is that woman still up a tree? I'm from Channel 5. We're sending a crew. Is that all right?"

"No," I said. "It's not all right."

"Pardon me?"

"I don't want you taking pictures of my mom acting dumb."

"What's your name? Can we interview you? How do you feel about what your mom is doing?"

I hung up without answering, but the phone rang again. "CBC Radio, here. We'd like to talk to the woman who's up the tree. Do you have a cell phone so she can do a phone interview?"

"No," I yelled. "We don't have a cell phone, and I wouldn't take it to her if we did."

"Are you her daughter? How do you feel about your mother's environmental statement?"

I hung up again, but the doorbell rang, probably someone else wanting to see the crazy mother who lived in a tree. I grabbed a piece of paper, ignoring the ringing.

Taking the fattest felt marker I could find, I printed in big, black letters: *Mother in tree around side of house. Don't ring doorbell. Don't bother me.* I drew an arrow pointing the way to the tree. The doorbell had stopped ringing, so I opened the door and stuck the sign on it. Then I went back in and closed the curtains in the living room so no one could see inside.

I heard another vehicle arrive and peeked out. The Channel 5 truck pulled up and people with cameras and other equipment got out. I pulled the curtains together again. I didn't want to talk to reporters from a TV station. I most certainly didn't want them to take my picture while they asked me how I felt about Mom being up a tree.

Why did everyone keep asking me how I felt? How did they expect me to feel? I felt rotten. I felt worried. I felt scared.

Worried about what I was going to feed Mom for lunch and dinner and breakfast the next day and the day after that and the day after that. Worried about who would buy the groceries when we ran out of milk and bread. Worried about how Mom was going to get to the bank, or pay for my swimming lessons, or book my flight to see Dad next month or do anything at all if she wasn't going to come down from that tree.

Scared she would fall and hurt herself.

And very very scared about what my friends would say when they found out what was going on.

How did I *feel*? What a dumb question.

Chapter Four

The Channel 5 people rang the door-bell in spite of my sign, but when I didn't open the door, they went around the side of the house. Peering through the curtains, I saw another TV truck arrive followed by two cars.

I grabbed a clean tin from the recy-cling, picked up the felt marker and popped outside again. At the beginning of my sign I wrote *50 cents to see*...in front of *Mother in tree*, and at the bottom I put *Leave money in tin.* I thought for a moment then added, *please.*

Fifty cents wasn't much, but if I had to buy the groceries, I had to earn some money. Mom wasn't going to sell any pottery while she was in the tree house. There would be lots of reporters coming. That meant I should collect enough money to buy milk and bread. Maybe there'd even be some money left over to rent that video Mom didn't want me to watch. She'd never know.

There were footsteps on the front stairs, then laughter. Money clinked into the tin, and the footsteps went away. Great! I thought. It worked.

I took another quick peek through the curtains. There were more people heading for the front door. They read the sign and paid up. I counted the clicks as they tossed money into the tin. Just like the circus,

I thought. I could almost hear the ring-master's voice, "Step right up, Ladies and Gentlemen. Only fifty cents buys you a look at the strange thing in a tree. The Mother from Mars. The Weirdest Mother on Earth. Ladies and Gentlemen, this is a sight you will never forget. Step right up. See the mother. See the tree."

See the clock. It was nearly ten o'clock, time for the press conference.

Well, I wasn't going to be at that press conference. No one had invited me and I didn't want to go, anyway.

The doorbell rang. I didn't answer it. It rang again, harder and longer, so I shouted, "Can't you read? Don't bother me."

Whoever it was didn't answer but kept their thumb on the doorbell so it kept on ringing and ringing. This was too much, I thought. I opened the door, ready to shout "Go away!" but all that came out was "G…G…G…Grandma!"

"Calendula Powers, does your mother

have any idea you are charging people to attend her press conference?"

My grandmother, Rose, stood on the front steps, with a suitcase beside her and my tin can in her hands. She looked angry, and she shook the tin so hard the quarters inside rattled.

"I am ashamed of you, Callie. Your mother will be mortified."

"What are you doing here, Grandma?"

"Didn't she tell you I was coming?" Grandma's voice got softer. "I'm sorry. You've spent the morning wondering how you were going to manage alone, haven't you?"

I nodded but didn't say anything. "Poor Callie. It's all right. I'm here to help. I told Dian I'd come."

I shrugged. "Mom didn't tell me anything. She never does," I said.

"Your mother's had a lot to think about, dear. This is a very brave thing she's doing."

"Brave? I think it's stupid."

"Nonsense. You should be proud of her, fighting to save that wonderful old tree and the tree house. I remember when your grandfather built it—it took him three weekends. Your mother and I slept in it the night it was finished. She wanted to spend the night in the tree house, but she was too scared to sleep there alone. We had hot chocolate in a thermos…"

Gran's voice trailed off, and I knew she was remembering the old days.

This was—and still is—Grandma's house. She and Grandpa lived here for years. After I was born, Mom and Dad and I lived with them until Dad left. When Grandpa died two years ago Gran said there were too many memories here, so she moved to an apartment across town. The other people in her building are mostly retired, and they play cards every afternoon. They don't like kids visiting even though there's a great pool.

"I'm glad you're here, Gran," I said, hugging her.

"Your mother needs help with that Harold Wilson," said Gran. "He never got over her, you know. I'm sure that's why he's…"

"Got *over* her? Mom? You mean they were…"

"Sort of engaged at one time. Yes. Until she met your father."

I suddenly wanted to sit down. "Mr. Wilson? But he's nearly bald."

"He's the same age as your mother, Callie. This happened a long time ago. However, now is not the time to discuss it. You and I have a press conference to attend."

"Not me! I'm not going."

"You most certainly are. Family support, that's what's needed. We'll show those people that the Powers women mean business."

"*We*?"

Grandma grabbed her suitcase. "Bring the other thing inside too," she told me.

The "other thing" turned out to be a small port-a-potty that folded up like plastic suitcases. Gross, I thought. However, it didn't smell and it looked clean, so I picked it up and carried it inside. Trust Grandma to think of bringing that.

I could hear the noise and laughter of the crowd gathered around the side of the house. Grandma opened the curtains, and I saw more people arrive. "Step right up," I said out loud. "Welcome to the Powers' family circus."

"This is not a circus, Callie. This is serious. Go wash your face so you, at least, will look presentable. I'm sure Dian looks terrible after spending half the night in that tree house."

"I don't want to go."

Grandma ignored me. "Do something with your hair too."

"I don't want my picture taken, so why do I have to…"

"Calendula, stop talking and get ready."

I sighed. There's no arguing with my grandma. Or with my mom. When they've made up their minds, that's it. It doesn't matter what *you* want; you do what *they* want. Or else.

"Powers Power." That's what my dad called it, that stubbornness. My grandma is Rose Powers. My mom kept her own last name when she got married so she's Dian Powers and I'm Calendula Evans Powers, but I'm not nearly as stubborn as Mom or Grandma. At least, I don't think I am.

Five minutes later, with my face washed and hair and teeth brushed, I followed my grandma out the front door.

Why me? I thought as we pushed our way to the front of the reporters. Why does she have to be my mother?

Chapter Five

It was very crowded in the narrow space between the fence and our house. People were packed in so tightly that no one could move. Cameras flashed and video recorders whirred. Mom waved at Gran and me. The reporters moved aside so we could stand under the tree.

Mom was sitting on a branch above our heads with her feet dangling down.

I could see the bottom of her running shoes if I looked up.

But I looked down instead. I stared at the ground and hoped my face wouldn't show in the pictures the photographers were taking.

"Let's begin," said Mom, and then the questions started.

"You're Dian Powers' daughter, right?"

"Who are you, ma'am? The kid's grandma?"

"How old are you?"

"None of your business, young man!" Grandma answered, but I think the reporter was actually talking to me.

"Age doesn't matter," Mom yelled. "We are together in this protest; three generations united to prevent a terrible wrong."

"Could we have your names, please?"

"Dianthus, Rose and Calendula," Mom said.

"Hey, those are all names of flowers! Like the women in that mystery show on TV," a reporter said.

"The women in my family have been named after flowers long before that silly TV series," said Grandma. "The writer probably stole the idea from us."

"What kind of flower is a calendula?" someone asked.

"A yellow or orange one, like a daisy," someone else answered.

"I wanted to name her Daffodil, but her father objected," said Mom.

Thank you Dad, I thought. What kind of a nickname would I have if my name was Daffodil? Even worse, they could have named me Snapdragon or Geranium after Aunt Gerry.

Peter Dawl looked surprised. "Daffodil?" he said to me. "She really wanted to name you Daffodil?"

I glared at him. "That's right, Ken."

He grinned. "Some people's moms."

"Hey, know what we've got here?" said someone. "It's 'Flower Power,' just like in the 1960s. It's a sit-in."

"More like a 'sit-up,'" said the CBC reporter, craning her neck to look up at Mom. Everyone laughed, and the cameras started flashing again.

"Flower Power? What's that?" I asked.

"Back in the sixties the hippies were called 'Flower Children.' They thought that love and peace should replace war. Flowers were a symbol of love, so they gave out flowers, wore flowered clothes and even had flower tattoos."

"That's dumb. Mom's not a hippie. They didn't wear shoes or take baths," I said. No one paid any attention to me. Everyone was leaning backward and shouting up at Mom.

"Are you making an environmental statement against all logging or is this a personal disagreement?"

"How old is this tree?"

"Will you sleep up there tonight?"

Peter Dawl shouted louder than the rest. "Who owns the tree house?"

"I do." Four people answered: Mom, Grandma, me and Mr. Wilson. I hadn't noticed him arrive, but there he was, hanging over the fence, glaring at everyone.

"My father made it for me," said Mom.

"My husband built it," said Grandma. "He bought the lumber. All Harold Wilson's father did was help, and not very much as I remember. The first thing he did was fall out of the tree and sprain his wrist."

"It's in *my* tree," said Mr. Wilson.

"I'm the only one who uses the tree house," I said. "It's mine."

"It's not. It's on my property. I can do what I want with it."

"No you can't," shouted Mom, but no one was listening. All the reporters were talking to Mr. Wilson.

"Why are you going to cut down the tree? Are you asserting your rights as a property owner? Would you consider changing your mind?"

"No, I won't change my mind. It's my tree. If that crazy woman is still up there tomorrow I'll call the police and have her arrested. She's trespassing."

"I am not! I'm on my side of the fence," yelled Mom.

"It's my tree," Mr. Wilson said again. "And it, the tree house and that woman in it are all coming down tomorrow morning. I have nothing else to say." He turned around and left. A few seconds later we heard a door slam as he went back inside his house.

Chapter Six

Mr. Wilson may not have had anything more to say, but everyone else did. The reporters asked questions, wrote things down and took pictures and video footage of us. That night our pictures were on the front page of the paper and on the television news. Mom couldn't watch TV because she was still up the tree, so Grandma and I taped the programs for her to watch later. Every hour on the hour the radio replayed Mom and Mr. Wilson shouting at each other. Mom was able to hear these reports on the radio Grandma had sent over in the basket. Even inside the house with the TV on, Grandma and I could hear Mom happily shouting, "Yes!" as she listened.

The TV stations had longer reports on the six o'clock evening news. We kept switching channels, but it seemed every news program mentioned us. There we were: Gran, me, Mom; and Mr. Wilson glowering over the fence. Some of the reporters were laughing as they explained what was going on. They all called it the "Flower Power Standoff."

What a stupid joke. You'd have to be Grandma's age to get it.

Gran in her red jogging outfit looked fine on TV, but I looked weird, as if I hadn't brushed my hair in days. I had on my orange T-shirt, and my hair looked the same color, though it isn't really that red. Mom wore a bright pink T-shirt with *save our forests* on it. You couldn't read what the lettering said because most of the pictures showed only her face or the chain around her ankle.

The CBC reporter went on and on about our names, "There they are, three women, three generations, each dressed in the color of the flower she is named for—bright pink Dianthus, vivid red Rose and brilliant orange Calendula. The vibrant colors they wear reflect the determination of these remarkable women who…"

She had more to say, but I stopped listening. Almost all of the reporters had used my full name! Now everyone—all the kids at school, and at swimming—everyone who knew me would know my real name was Calendula. If I'd felt embarrassed before, I was close to dying or running away from home by the time the newscasts were over.

Although we'd turned off the ringer on the phone, the answering machine had been busy all day. While Grandma was getting supper ready—real macaroni and cheese, not the stuff in a box—we listened to the messages.

There were messages from reporters, from Mom's friends at the Art Society and from my best friend, Josie.

"Is Calendula really your name?" she asked. "How come you never told me? What's 'Flower Power'? What is your mom doing this time, Callie? Can I come over tonight? Can I be on TV too?"

I phoned her back. "Yes, because, never mind, never mind, no and no."

"Huh?"

"I just answered all your questions, Josie. Don't come over. It's weird here."

"But, Calendula—"

"Don't call me that, Josephine!"

"Sorry. Why can't I come over? I'm your best friend. I want to be on TV with you."

"Some friend you are," I said. "Here's my mom being really stupid and all you can talk about is getting on TV. If you can't think of a way to help me, just stay away…"

"That's not fair. I only want to—"

I snapped at her. "Not fair? I'll tell you what's not fair. Everyone in the whole world is looking at me, and my mom and my gran, and laughing at us. If that happened to you, I'd feel sorry for you. I'd try to help."

"But Callie, how can I help if I can't come over?"

"Just stay away, Josie," I said again. "You're the lucky one. You *can* stay away."

That was something I'd like to do too. Stay away from this crazy business, and from reporters who told the whole world my real name and laughed at my mother.

Maybe, I thought, I'd call Josie back and see if I could go to her house. But I knew I couldn't do that, not with Grandma here. She'd never let me go. I needed to show—what was it Gran had said—"family support." I decided I should stay. After all, this was my house, and that woman in the tree outside was my mother. Weird or not, this house and this mother were mine and I'd have to stay with them both.

Finally the day ended. It had been a very very long day. When it was completely dark, Grandma cautiously opened the front door and peered outside. Then she went to the back porch and looked around. "They've all gone," she said.

"They'll be back," I sighed. "Mom will make sure of that."

"Yes, they will be back," said Grandma, "but for now it's quiet. Callie, go and sit on the front porch. Whistle if someone comes."

"Whistle? What shall I whistle?"

"The tune to a song. Or pretend you're calling a dog."

"We don't have a—"

"I know that. Just make a noise. Anything, but do it loudly. I need a lookout."

"But—"

"Calendula! Just do it."

Gran had the same tone in her voice Mom uses, the one that means "or else," so I turned off the front porch light and crept outside. I didn't want anyone to see me. I'd been seen enough. I sat on the bench swing and pushed myself back and forth, listening to the night bugs chirping away as I batted at mosquitoes.

Inside, I heard laughter. Then the upstairs shower started. When the water stopped running, I heard voices in the kitchen and I knew that Mom was out of the tree house.

There's a board under my bed that's long enough to reach out my bedroom window to the tree. At one end there are two big metal hooks. If you put the hooks around a branch of the tree, and rest the other end on the window ledge, it becomes a bridge. You can also get to the tree house by using a ladder that's nailed into the tree trunk, but that's on Mr. Wilson's side of the fence. From our side, the only way to get into the tree house is by using the board through my window.

It's the same board Mom had when she was a kid. My room used to be hers. She said that sometimes she'd climb out to the tree house then shinny down the tree when she was supposed to be grounded. I never understood why Grandma hadn't taken the board away.

Maybe she never found out that Mom had sneaked out. I'd thought about using the board the last time I was grounded, but I had nowhere to go, so I stayed in my room.

Mom used the board bridge to come across to the house, just like she used to do when she was a kid. No one could have seen her in the dark, even if there were someone around. Mr. Wilson could have seen her, if he'd looked out one of his upstairs windows, but he wasn't home. I'd seen him climb on his bike earlier to go for a ride. His house was dark and empty, and I knew I'd be able to hear that noisy motorcycle coming long before he got here.

I thought about whistling something, just to make Mom and Grandma nervous. I had been out there an hour, swinging and thinking about whistling, when Gran finally called, "You can come in now, Callie."

"Did you and Mom have a good time? Did she enjoy her dinner? How come she came down from the tree, anyway?"

Grandma didn't answer me. "Isn't Mom supposed to be doing a sit-in or a sit-up? She said she was going to stay there until Mr. Wilson changed his mind, so why did she come in for a shower? Isn't that cheating?"

Grandma looked surprised. "If anyone asks, you didn't see her leave the tree. It's been hot today and she needed a shower."

"So I don't lie, I just don't tell the whole truth?" I asked. "That's not right."

"Just say what you saw. Or didn't see," said Gran.

"You didn't answer me. Am I supposed to lie? How come grown-ups can lie anytime they want to, but they tell their kids not to?"

"Calendula, that's enough," said Gran. Her voice had Mom's "or else" tone again. "You don't have to tell anyone anything because you didn't see anything. Probably no one will ask you anyway. Now go to bed. Tomorrow will be a busy day."

I thought about saying I wasn't tired, but actually I was. Very tired. So I went upstairs, brushed my teeth and splashed water on my face, then went to my room and stuck my head out the window.

"Night, Mom. Sleep tight."

"Good night, Callie. Don't worry. We'll win this fight."

"We?" I said. "Does it have to be 'we'?"

"We're in this together, Calendula. Now, turn off that overhead light—it shines right in my eyes. Go to sleep. Remember, I'll know if you're reading in bed. I can see your bedside light."

I pulled my head back in and yanked down the blind.

"I can still see the light, Callie."

"I'll just read for a few minutes, Mom."

"No, you won't. Turn off that light and go to bed. It's late."

I sighed again. I'd done a lot of sighing today. "Okay, Mom," I said.

It wasn't going to be easy having her staring into my room all day and night. But there wasn't anything I could do about it.

I turned out both of my lights and climbed into bed. Maybe Mom would change her mind, I thought. Maybe it would be hot and buggy in the tree tonight. Maybe the chain would hurt her ankle.

Maybe, just maybe, when I woke up in the morning I'd find her in the kitchen, talking to Gran and drinking tea, and all of this would be over.

But, knowing my mom, it wouldn't be over—not this soon, not this easily. I sighed one last time and shut my eyes.

Chapter Seven

The next morning, before I was fully awake, I heard voices downstairs. "Mom!" I thought happily. "She came down from the tree!"

Then it began again, just like the day before. *Scritch, scritchy-scratch* on the window, and Mom calling me.

I rolled out of bed and went to the window. Mom grinned. "I'm ready for the big day, or will be as soon as I have my breakfast," she said. "Go downstairs and tell your grandmother I'm hungry."

"She's busy," I said. "She's got company."

"I know," said Mom. "I saw them arrive. Maybe she'll make pancakes. I'm starving."

I pulled on the clothes I'd worn the day before and went downstairs to the kitchen.

"Good morning," said my grandma.

"Good morning," chorused six other grandmas. I blinked and looked again. At least I thought they were grandmas. They were all about my gran's age, and they all wore long skirts and huge hats. On every hat was a flower. Or a lot of flowers.

I started back upstairs. There were too many grandmas to face first thing in the morning. "Callie, come back here," called my gran. "Come and meet my friends."

Reluctantly, I turned around, noticing for the first time that my grandma was also wearing a hat. She still was in my grandfather's old blue dressing gown, but on top of her head was a huge hat with what looked like a whole rose garden on it.

"These are the Singing Grannies, Callie," my gran said. "They've come to help. Look at the beautiful hat they brought me."

I guess I was still half asleep, because I knew, the moment I said it, that the words shouldn't have left my mouth. "Help? How can they help? They're grandmas."

"Calendula! No one is too old for anything. Not unless they feel old, and these ladies are young at heart. They sing at protests all over the country. They're always on TV."

"Sing? TV?"

"Let's show her," said my grandma, and the Singing Grannies clumped together looking like a popcorn ball sprinkled with flowers. To the tune of "This Land is My Land" they sang, "This tree's a good tree, a very fine tree, please leave it standing, don't cut it down."

They started on the second verse, but suddenly Gran rushed to the stove. "My pancakes!"

The other Grannies went to help her, flapping their hats at the cloud of black smoke coming from the frying pan.

"Mom wants her breakfast," I said. "I'll just—uh—I'll just go back upstairs. Okay?"

No one was paying any attention to me or to the person knocking loudly on the back door. I decided to ignore the knocking too, and started sneaking away, but then the answering machine cut in. We hadn't turned the ringer back on the night before, and with all the singing and flapping going on I hadn't noticed the answering machine pick up. The voice coming from the machine was very loud. It was my father.

"Callie? What's happening? I just turned on the TV. Pick up the phone. I know you're there. The weather channel is showing a picture of the house and your mother. Why is she chained to the maple tree?"

"Talk to your father, Callie," said my gran. She rushed to the living room window and looked out. "He's right. The reporters are here already. I wonder how long they've been filming? Quickly, girls, get out there. The cameras are rolling."

"Good morning," said Peter Dawl as he pushed open the back door and walked into our kitchen. "Excuse me, I knocked, but nobody answered."

I picked up the phone, stopping the answering machine. "Now is not a good time, Dad."

"I gathered that, Callie. What is your mother up to—besides the tree?"

"Oh, just the regular, you know. She's upset, so she's going to do something about it and…"

"Oh, Callie, not again. Are you all right? Do you want to come out here? I can get you on a plane this afternoon. School's nearly over. You wouldn't miss much if you came to Ottawa early, would you?"

When Dad and Mom split up, he moved to Ottawa. I spend half of my summer holidays with him, usually the first half. But he's got a new wife and three-year-old twins now.

I started to say, "Yes, I'd love to come," but then I remembered how awkward I'd felt the last few times I'd visited. The twins were cute, I guess, but Dad was always "ooohing" and "aaahing" over them and talking baby talk. The last time he picked me up at the airport he had a streak of baby barf down the front of his shirt, and he hadn't even noticed.

Dad and I use to do things together during my visits. We would walk along the river, go to these funny little restaurants and to movies. He took me shopping and let me buy all sorts of clothes that Mom wouldn't let me wear at home. But now Dad stays home and crawls around on the floor with the babies, and the only shows we watch are Teletubbies videos. When we do go out, we all have to go—twins, strollers, diaper bag…

"No, thanks, Dad," I said. "I'll stay here. I think Mom needs me."

"I'm sure she does," said my father.

"I'm sure she does," said Peter Dawl, who had been listening to my side of the conversation with my dad. "She was hollering for breakfast."

"Of course she needs you," said my Grandmother. "She needs you to take her some food, Callie. Toast and a thermos of tea—I don't have time for pancakes now that the press has arrived. Use the sugar substitute and the reduced-calorie jam I saw in the fridge; your mother's put on a bit of weight lately. I have to rush. I need to get dressed."

"Callie?" said my father into the phone. "Callie, what's happening? Is that your grandmother's voice? Is she there?"

"Everybody's here, Dad. Not just one grandma, a whole bouquet of them."

"What?"

"Never mind. You'll see them on TV soon."

"Callie, what on earth is going on? Are you all right?"

"I'm fine, Dad. Really," I said. "It's just Mom. And Grandma. You know."

He groaned. "I know. I know very well. Listen, call me anytime. And if you change your mind about coming out to Ottawa early this summer…"

"No, Dad, it's okay. I'll phone you later. Right now, I've got to go."

Someone else was banging on the back door. Peter Dawl answered it. "Please respect the family's privacy," he said. "Join the other reporters outside. You can ask questions at a more suitable time."

"Who told you to say that?" I asked.

"Hey, I figured you could use the help," he said. "If you don't want me here, I'll leave."

"What are you doing here, anyway? I mean, inside. I didn't invite you."

He blushed. "Well, the door was unlocked. I thought that, because I'm from the neighborhood paper, not the national television stations or the big newspapers, maybe you could ask your mom to give me an exclusive."

"What does that mean?"

"That she talks to me without the other reporters around. A one-on-one interview."

"Why would she do that?"

"If you asked her to, she might."

"Why would I ask her?"

He grinned at me. "Because my mother wanted to name me Ken and your mother wanted to name you Daffodil."

I thought for a moment. "Okay, Ken. Here's the deal. You make toast and tea for Mom's breakfast and you stop anyone else from coming in. Then see if you can get my Gran to take off that silly hat, and I'll ask Mom to give you an exclusive."

"It's a deal," he said. "Except for the hat part. Your grandma scares me."

I knew what he meant.

"But why toast?" he went on. "Isn't that a bowl of pancake batter? You like pancakes, Daffy?"

"Sure," I said, but he didn't hear me. No one could have heard anything at all because a roar of noise filled the street. The house shook and the glasses in the cupboards clinked together.

Gran was halfway up the stairs, but she ran back down. Peter and I followed her to the living room. She pulled open the curtains, and we all looked outside.

A dozen or more huge motorbikes, their chrome glistening in the sun, their engines roaring, were cruising slowly down the street.

I wasn't at all surprised when they stopped in front of our house.

Chapter Eight

"Oh, dear," said my grandmother. "I do hope there isn't going to be trouble."

I stared at her in amazement. "We've already got trouble, Gran," I said. "Remember? Mom chained to the tree and all of that?"

But Gran wasn't listening. "Look! They're getting off their bikes! They're coming over here!"

A huge biker with a gut that hung over the top of his leather pants and stretched the edges of his open vest, pulled a piece of paper from his pocket. He looked at the paper, then at our house.

He looked at the paper again, then scratched his armpit and led the other bikers into Harold Wilson's front yard.

"They aren't coming to our house," said my gran. "I am relieved."

"This isn't a bikers' neighborhood," said Peter. "Why are they here?"

The doorbell rang. Gran pulled her robe more tightly around her. "Maybe those men are coming to our house after all," she said nervously. "I'd better answer the door and send them away. I do wish I were properly dressed."

I headed back to the kitchen, wondering what well-dressed grandmas wore to welcome bikers. I heard the front door open, then Gran's voice greeting someone. "Oh. It's just one of your little friends, Callie."

Why does she always have to call them little? All my friends are as tall as I am or taller. I went back to the front hall to see which midget friend had come to visit.

"Hi, Callie," said Josie.

"What are you doing here, Josie? I told you not to come."

Gran frowned. "Be polite, Calendula," she said. "Now, you and your little friend only have time for a short visit. Don't forget to take your mother her breakfast, then come outside and join us. We need your support." She tossed her head, making the roses on her hat bounce, and went upstairs to get dressed.

Josie came inside and shut the door. "Cool bikes. Are those guys visiting you?"

"Go home, Josie," I said, turning away and heading back to the kitchen again. "I don't want any visitors."

She sounded hurt. "Not even me?" she asked. "Your best friend?"

"My best friend doesn't care about me," I said. "She just wants to be on TV."

"That's not true," Josie said, following me. "I want to help. Look: I brought money."

"What for? I don't need money."

"It's not for you," she said. "Some of the kids in our class went on a bottle drive last night, after we saw you on TV. We made thirty-five dollars and ten cents."

"Good for you."

"It's for your neighbor, Mr. Wilson. We thought if we gave him the money he wouldn't cut the tree down."

"You can't buy a tree for thirty-five dollars and ten cents," I said. "That's stupid."

"No, it's not. I think it's a great idea," said Peter Dawl. "Callie, why don't I make you and your friend some pancakes? While you eat she can tell me about how your schoolmates are helping with the protest."

"He's going to ask you for an exclusive."

"It would be a good story," the reporter said. "Environmentally conscious school friends help…"

"We're not environmentalists!" said Josie. "We just want to be on TV."

"Pay no attention to him, then," I said. "He's only a newspaper reporter."

Peter Dawl looked up from the bowl of pancake batter he was stirring. He'd found Mom's pink apron and tied it around his waist. "Don't say 'only,' please," he said. "Newspaper reporters are important too. Everyone reads the newspaper, especially a local paper like the *Tribune*. Tell me about your bottle drive, Josie."

Josie shook her head. "Thanks, but I'd rather talk to the TV reporters. I'll go get some of the other kids.

Maybe the TV people will take our picture."

"Why don't you talk to me?" said Peter. "I've got a camera."

"We'll try the TV people first," Josie said. "But if they don't want to take our picture, then I guess you can."

"Thanks a lot," he said. Peter was being sarcastic, but Josie didn't get it.

"You really are generous today, aren't you?" I said to her.

"I'm trying to help," she said. "I don't know why you're in such a bad mood, Calendula."

She used my full name. She wasn't in a good mood either. "Shut the door behind you," I snarled. Then I turned to the reporter. "Did you say something about pancakes? I'm hungry."

"Oh, I almost forgot," said Josie, sticking her head back into the kitchen. "I went around the side of the house and talked to your mom before I rang the bell. She wants her breakfast."

"Goodbye, Josephine," I said and she left. I heard the front door close behind her.

"I forgot about Mom's breakfast. She's probably mad. She's got blood sugar problems and gets cranky if she doesn't eat."

"Give me five minutes," said Peter.

I made tea and filled the thermos while he flipped pancakes. They smelled good.

When everything was ready, he turned off the stove. "Wait until I get my camera, and we'll take your mom her breakfast. How do you get food to her, by the way?"

"It's a secret," I said, not wanting a picture of my room, which wasn't very tidy, in the next *Westside Tribune*. "I'll do it. Alone."

He looked disappointed. "Okay, but remember to ask her about my exclusive."

I didn't get a chance to ask Mom anything. "Where have you been, Callie?" she asked. "Do you know why all those bikers are in Harold's back-yard? Hurry and send my breakfast over. I could kill for a cup of tea."

I put the plastic containers and the big thermos in the basket and swung it over to her. She didn't even say thank you. She just popped the lid off the largest container and grabbed a pancake.

"Brush your hair, Callie, and come outside. Another van from a TV station— oh, good, it's CBC—just pulled up in the lane. Hurry so we can do our family interview."

"Not yet, Mom. I need my break-fast too, you know. I'll be there soon. If I have to."

"You have to," said Mom though a mouthful of pancake. "Of course you have to."

I guess I did have to, even though I didn't want to. I went back downstairs where Peter Dawl was at the back door talking to someone. "Yes Ma'am, I'll do it, but I'd like to get out of the kitchen soon. I'm a reporter, you know, not a cook."

He shut the door. "Your grandmother is organizing me. On her way outside to join the Singing Grannies she demanded—excuse me, requested—that I make coffee. Doesn't she realize I have a breaking story to cover?"

"Breaking?"

"That's reporter talk for something that's happening right now. Did your mom agree to an exclusive?"

"She wants to eat before she decides," I said. "Can I have breakfast too?"

"Sure," he said and pulled a plate of pancakes out of the oven. "Where's the coffee? And the coffee pot?"

I ate while he started the coffee. "Good pancakes. Thanks."

"You're welcome," he said. "Your grandmother's batter was a bit thick, so I added some more milk and an egg. They are good, aren't they?" He picked one up from the plate and bit into it. "Very good, if I do say so myself."

He took off the apron and tried to brush down his hair with his hands, but his hair didn't look any better when he finished. As a matter of fact, it looked worse. There was a streak of pancake mix in it now that looked like gross yellow hair gel. I decided not to mention it.

"Time for me to get to work," he said. "You coming out?"

I sighed the first sigh of the day. "I guess so. Mom said I had to."

Swallowing the last bite of pancake, I stood up and took a deep breath.

Peter Dawl looked at me. "I know," he said. "Mothers. It's hard to live with them, but..."

"But what?"

"My mom died last year," he said. "Cancer."

I didn't know what to say. "Sorry," I finally blurted out.

"Thank you," he said, and his eyes went misty. "I never thought I'd miss her this much. She was a terror. Always telling me what to do. Getting involved in all kinds of clubs and organizations, then dragging me to their meetings and making me write about them for the paper. Telling me what to wear and that it was time I got married. Introducing me to really odd girls she met at meetings and..." He shrugged. "Anyway, your mom reminds me of my mother, so I'm going to support her. Even if she doesn't give me an exclusive, I can still write a good article, which might help win her fight to save that tree. You coming?"

I thought for a moment. Mom did some crazy things and sometimes I wished I didn't have to live with her, but what if she were dead like Peter's mom? That would be awful. I would miss her, even more than I had missed my dad when he first left. Maybe what she was doing to save the tree wasn't so stupid. Maybe I shouldn't be embarrassed. Maybe I should be…

"Are you coming?" Peter asked again.

"Yes," I said. "I'm ready."

"Really?"

"No, but I have to go out there."

His face was serious. "Yes," he said. "I'm afraid you do."

Chapter Nine

Peter opened the kitchen door, and we stepped out onto the back porch.

The Grannies were singing away, my gran stood in front waving her arms around like a conductor. Flowers bounced happily on all of the Grannies' hats, keeping time to the music. There were a lot of reporters in the lane.

They were hanging over the back fence, shoving and pushing each other.

Everyone in the lane seemed to have cameras or microphones. When Peter and I appeared on the back porch, all the cameras started flashing and clicking and whirring, like a bunch of crazy fireflies that don't know they aren't supposed to be around in the daylight.

"Why are all the reporters over in the lane?" I asked him. "Yesterday they were right in our yard."

"I told them to stay off your property," said Peter.

"You told them? Why would they do anything you told them to?"

"I sort of let them think I was family."

"What kind of family?"

"Your family. Your uncle," he admitted.

"You lied!"

"Not exactly."

I sighed again. It wasn't even nine o'clock and already I'd sighed twice. "Just what I need," I said. "More family. So, Uncle Ken, are you going to climb the tree and join Mom or are you going to put on a flower hat and sing with Grandma?"

He looked indignant. "Neither. I made breakfast, didn't I? That's my contribution for the day. That and the coffee. You can also thank me for the fact that no reporters have been knocking on your door this morning."

"No reporters except you," I pointed out.

I went to the edge of the porch and peered around the side of the house. I could see the tree; I could see Mom perched in it. Sunlight filtered down through the branches and glinted off the chain around her ankle. She waved at me.

"Hi, Callie."

"Hi, Mom. How was your breakfast?"

"It was great, thank your grandma for me."

"Actually Uncle Ken made it."

I don't think she heard me, because she just smiled and waved again and didn't ask who Uncle Ken was. She looked cheerful, which was good. Her blood sugar must have evened itself out.

From the porch, I could see into Harold Wilson's backyard. The bikers, with Mr. Wilson in the middle, were staring up at Mom.

Mr. Wilson wasn't wearing a leather vest like the rest of his friends. He wore jeans and a baseball cap that covered up the bald spot on the top of his head. He saw me and called out, "Callie! Can't you talk some sense into your mother?"

I laughed. "You're kidding, right?"

"This has gone on long enough. The tree removal people will be here any minute, and that tree is coming down even if your mom is still in it."

"Not on your life, Harold," yelled my mom. "This tree stays. Who are all those badly dressed men in your yard, anyway? Are they going to help you take me out of this tree?"

"They're members of my bike club—my new friends," he answered. "They've come to support me and, yes, I'm sure they'd love to pull you out of the tree."

"I'd like to see them try!" said my gran.

"You and those old ladies in hats think you can stop them?" asked Mr. Wilson. "Who *are* the women in your yard anyway, Dian?"

"They're the Singing Grannies," my grandmother answered. "They're famous."

The biker with the big stomach laughed. "Hey, so that's what that noise is? Singing? I thought it was a bunch of coyotes howling."

The Grannies moved into the narrow passageway between Mr. Wilson's fence and our house. They glared across the fence at the bikers. "Let's show them how these coyotes can howl, girls," one of them said. "Lots of volume, now."

She counted, "One, two, three," and the Grannies began singing again, louder this time, "This tree's a good tree, a very fine tree, please leave it standing, don't cut it down."

In Mr. Wilson's yard, the bikers moved closer to the fence. They scowled at the Grannies. The Grannies sang louder.

"Hey," said the biker with the big gut. "We can sing better than that." He scratched his head for a moment, thinking. "How about this?"

To the tune of "Twinkle, Twinkle Little Star" he sang, "Bikers, bikers stand as one, cut this tree down for some fun."

"Fun?" shouted my mother. "You call the death of a tree fun? You insensitive louts."

"We prefer not to be referred to as louts, Ma'am," said a tall skinny biker with lots of gray hair in a ponytail, a gray beard and wraparound sunglasses. "But she's right, that's a pretty awful song, Duke. The tune's catchy, but the words suck."

Duke pulled his shoulders straight and his large stomach quivered. "So, make up your own song, if you think you can do better."

"Okay." The gray-haired biker pushed his glasses up on the top of his head. For a while he was quiet, then he grinned and pulled his glasses back down. "How about this?" he said. He took a deep breath and in a voice like an opera singer, he sang, "Crazy lady stand aside, we'll take this tree down then we'll ride."

"Who's crazy?" shouted my mom. "You are. You're grown-ups who still play with toys."

"Toys? You calling our machines 'toys'?" said Duke.

"This tree's a good tree, a very fine tree...," sang the Grannies.

"Crazy lady stand aside...," boomed the bikers. Almost all of them were singing now. They were louder than the Grannies, but they didn't stay with the tune very well. I don't think anyone would have recognized "Twinkle, Twinkle Little Star" the way the bikers sang it.

"This tree's a good tree..."

"...take this tree down, then we'll ride."

In spite of all the noise the two choirs were making, I could hear the reporters yelling.

"What's going on? What's happening? Can we get closer? I need shots for the news at noon. We want to interview Dian."

"I'd almost forgotten the reporters," said Mom. "Callie, tell them to come into the yard. They can't see what's going on from back there. Invite them in."

"Do I have to?" I asked no one in particular. I knew the answer to that question even before I asked it, so I pushed my way past bobbing flower hats and long skirts and went to the back gate.

"Hey, some of you reporters come into *this* yard," called Duke. "We want our pictures taken too, doing good stuff with our buddy Harold."

"Good stuff?" said my mother. "You believe helping that man cut down this tree is good stuff? I suppose you think that eating babies for breakfast is also a fine thing to do?"

"Babies? I didn't say nothing about babies, did I?"

"You can come in," I said to the reporters. Then I shouted it, so they could hear me. "You can come in. If you have to." I swung the gate open.

They stampeded past me, pushing the Grannies aside as they tried to get under the branches that hung over into our yard. Some of them rushed into Mr. Wilson's backyard while Duke held the gate open for them, smiling and trying to keep his belly tucked under his vest.

"Come in," he said. "We're protecting this citizen's right to do what he wants with his property. You can take our pictures too. We're good bikers doing good stuff. Make sure you write that down, okay?"

My head hurt. All the singing, the shouting, the reporters trying to talk to everyone and everyone trying to talk back all at once—it was just too much.

I decided to go back inside. It would be quieter there. Maybe no one would notice that I had gone. I thought there were a few pancakes left too. I could zap them in the microwave and...

Quickly, I slipped up the back stairs, across the porch and into the kitchen, shutting the door behind me.

At last I was alone and it was quiet—or sort of quiet. I could still hear the singing, especially the bikers. But no one was asking me to do anything and no one was trying to take my picture. I opened the oven door, looking for the plate of pancakes.

"Smile." A camera flashed.

Chapter Ten

"You blinked. Smile, Daffy, and I'll take another shot."

"Don't call me that, Ken. Who invited you back inside, anyway?"

"Your grandmother. She sent me to get the coffee for the Grannies."

"So get it and go."

He pointed the camera at me again. "Smile," he said again.

"Don't take my picture."

As he lowered the camera, he sighed. "I'd hoped you'd give me an interview. No one else will. They're all too busy talking to the TV crews and the reporters from the other newspapers. But you'll talk to me, right?"

"Wrong."

"Come on, Callie. Remember the pancakes?" He didn't call me Daffy this time. "I've got to write a story and I don't have any information. At least, no information that every other reporter doesn't already have. Talk to me. Tell me something about your mother. About your grandmother. Give me some background information, something exclusive."

"No." I wasn't going to tell him anything about our family. It was bad enough that everyone knew my full name and had seen pictures of my mom chained to the tree. I wasn't going to tell a reporter anything else. My friends already had enough to laugh at.

Peter put the camera down on the kitchen counter, took his glasses off and began cleaning them with the bottom of his T-shirt.

"Please, Callie. I really need a story. Help me out." Without his glasses he looked young, so young that I wondered if this was his first job. If he didn't get a good story to write for his newspaper, maybe he'd be fired. I tried not to feel sorry for him.

"I'll call Josie for you," I offered. "Maybe you can do that exclusive with her. About the bottle drive."

"Too late," he said. "The CBC television people and the *Globe and Mail* journalists have already grabbed her. See for yourself."

I peered out kitchen window. Josie and about six of my friends were perched on the garage roof. They had their backs to me, but I recognized Josie's long black hair. I couldn't see the reporters interviewing Josie and the other kids, but I guessed they were standing below the garage, taking pictures and scribbling notes. That night's news program would show a row of dangling feet and smiling faces. Josie would be happy. She'd made it onto the TV screen.

"What's that big piece of cardboard they're waving about?" I asked.

"It's a check. It's done with felt pens like the big pretend checks they give lottery winners."

"They made a giant check for thirty-five dollars and ten cents? You're kidding."

"Nope. It would have made a good exclusive. They're all neighborhood kids and the *Westside Tribune* is a neighborhood paper. How'd they get up on the roof anyway?"

"They climbed up the cherry tree beside the garage," I said. "It has branches that hang out over the lane. Mom keeps on saying they have to be cut back. Kids are always on the garage roof when the cherries are ripe. She's afraid someone will fall and she'll be responsible. She doesn't even use…"

"What doesn't she use?"

"Never mind," I said. "It's just a thought I had."

"Telling me about a cherry tree isn't the sort of background information that will help me with a story about the maple tree," said Peter. "But you're on the right track. Talk to me. Tell me how much the tree house means to you, or…"

I almost felt sorry enough for him to begin talking, but I was saved when the doorbell rang again.

"Didn't you tell all the reporters to stay away from the house?" I asked.

"Yes, I did," he answered. "But I guess this bunch didn't get the message. I'll go and send them away."

Because I wanted to hear how he pretended he was part of my family without actually lying, I followed him to the front door. I wouldn't mind knowing how to do the same thing—lie without telling an untruth. It would be a useful skill. For example, I could let Mom think I got an *A* on a science project without actually lying about the fact that I only got a *C*. Or I could let her believe that I was at the library, when I'd been at the mall.

"Uncle Ken" swung the door open, scowling, and was scowled back at by two policemen.

Quickly, the reporter's scowl changed to a smile. "How can I help you, officers?" he asked.

"We understand that the resident at this address is holding a protest. We came to make sure the permit is in order."

"Permit?" said Peter. "Of course. Yes. The permit."

I could tell he hadn't any idea what the policeman was talking about. I didn't either. Permit? What permit?

"There also seems to be a biker rally going on."

"You're mistaken, officers. There aren't any bikers here."

The policemen didn't say anything, but one of them turned and pointed silently at the dozen motorcycles parked in front of our house.

"Oh, those. They belong to friends of the next-door neighbor," said Peter.

"We need to check this house anyway, sir. This was the address the dispatcher gave us. Can you please show us the permit?"

"This isn't a real protest," said Peter. "Not the kind you need to get a permit for. There's just some grannies, some reporters, me and Daffy."

"Daffy?" asked one of the policemen.

"Grannies?" asked the other one.

"Don't call me that, Ken," I hissed.

"I mean, Callie, officers. She and her mother live here. Everyone else is just visiting."

"Everyone else?"

"The Grannies," I explained. "They're in the backyard. Singing."

I didn't really need to explain the singing. "This tree's a good tree, a very fine tree…" echoed from around the side of the house.

"Where is your mother, miss?" asked one of the policemen.

"She's up the—"

"She's outside," interrupted Peter. "There's no need for you to be here, officers. Everything's fine."

"Bikers, bikers stand as one…" I recognized that voice. It belonged to Duke, the biker with the large stomach. He was singing alone, loudly. He must have decided his song was better than the one the gray-haired biker had made up.

"Did you hear that?" one policeman asked the other.

"It sounds like the beginning of a riot. We need to check out this house, sir— and ma'am." My grandma had flounced into the front hall.

"Where's the coffee?" she asked Peter, and then she saw the policemen.

"Good morning, officers," she said, smiling and nodding her head so that the roses on her hat bounced up and down again. "Are you here to make those rude bikers leave?"

"If they're on your property, ma'am, we can ask them to vacate the premises."

"Oh, I guess this is my property. But I don't live here. My daughter does. I live across town."

"Is your daughter the one who organized the protest, ma'am?"

"Of course. She's the one up the tree," said Gran proudly.

"Up the what?" said a policeman, looking bewildered. I guess he hadn't watched the news last night.

"She's quite safe. But thank you for your concern."

"Ma'am, your daughter needs a permit to hold a protest," said one of the policemen. "Otherwise it's illegal."

"Oh, no, officers, Harold Wilson's the one who's illegal. I'm sure it's against the law to cut down trees in the city, but he's going to do it anyway. And he invited his biker friends to help him."

"The bikers," said a policeman. "I'd almost forgotten about them."

"How could you?" I asked. All the bikers were now singing "Bikers, bikers stand as one..." They were singing it loudly and off-key.

"I think we need backup," said the policeman to his partner. "Sounds as if there's a lot of bikers back there. Call it in. I'll check out the house."

One of the policemen headed for the patrol car that was parked in the middle of the road, its lights flashing.

"This way, officer," said Gran to the other policeman. "You can come through the kitchen to the back deck. From there you can see everything. Then you can arrest Harold Wilson and his nasty biker friends." She turned to Peter. "Young man, please hurry with the coffee. Bring a jug of water too. Singing is thirsty work."

Uncle Ken grumbled something I couldn't quite hear, and then followed Gran and the policeman. I think he regretted making himself an honorary member of my family.

I knew exactly how he felt. Today I also regretted belonging to this family. If I were only an honorary member, like Uncle Ken, I would decline the honor.

Through the open front door, I saw the policeman at the patrol car talking into his radio. How many more policemen were going to show up at my house, I wondered?

Then suddenly I was frightened. Not for myself. Frightened for Mom.

What had that policeman said about a permit? What did he mean about it being illegal to hold a protest without one?

Mom didn't have a permit, I was sure of that. She had climbed up the tree the same night that Mr. Wilson said he was going to cut it down. There hadn't been time for her to go to the police station or city hall or wherever you got permits.

Maybe when the police saw what Mom was doing, they'd arrest her.

I wanted her to come down from the tree, but I didn't want her to come down from the tree and go directly to jail.

I didn't think that was what my mother had in mind, either.

Chapter Eleven

I headed for my room. I had to talk to Mom, and if I spoke to her through my bedroom window, no one else would hear what I said. I had to tell her that the police had arrived. Let her know that she needed a permit to chain herself to the tree. Let her know that she was in trouble, serious trouble—getting arrested and going to jail kind of trouble.

I'd tell Mom a lie too. I'd tell her that I didn't care about the tree house anymore and that the tree's branches made my room too dark. I'd tell her I'd like it better if the sunlight could come into my room.

Maybe I'd beg her to come down.

Maybe I'd cry at her when I begged. I felt like crying. It wouldn't be hard to make the tears real.

I opened the window and stuck my head out.

"Hey, Mom."

"Callie! What are you doing in there? I told the reporter from CBC that you'd talk to her about..."

The urge to cry vanished. "I don't want to talk to anyone."

She looked surprised. "But your friends are being interviewed. Wasn't that sweet of them to take up a collection to save the tree?"

"I think it was stupid."

"Now, Callie, that's rude. You should have seen Josie offering that cardboard check to Harold and asking him if they could buy the tree. It was so cute."

In spite of myself, I was curious.

"What did Mr. Wilson say?"

"He growled at them and said he'd use the money to pay to have the tree cut down."

"Josie didn't give Mr. Wilson the money, did she?"

"Of course not."

"Good for Josie," I said. "First she gets to be on TV and now she's got an extra thirty-five dollars to spend."

"Don't be ridiculous, Calendula. You know the money isn't for her. Now, go down and talk to the reporters."

"What? I can't hear you, Mom. Those bikers are really noisy, aren't they?"

"Callie, you heard me perfectly well. Come outside."

"What's that? Okay, Mom, I'll bring you some coffee if there's any left."

"I didn't say coffee, I said come outside, and you know exactly what I..."

As I shut the window I realized I wasn't going to have that conversation with Mom after all. She wouldn't listen to me, no matter what I said. She'd just tell me to come outside and be interviewed.

I wasn't going. And Mom couldn't make me. Nor could all the Singing Grannies or the bikers.

Well, the bikers would be able to get me out of the house, but first they'd have to get in and catch me. I could still hear Grandma and Peter in the kitchen, clinking mugs as they got the coffee ready. As soon as they left I planned to lock the back door, put on my head-phones and crank my CD player up as high as it would go.

No one else was coming into this house, and I wasn't going out.

Plugged into my music, I wouldn't be able to hear anyone calling me or ringing the doorbell or anything.

Mom was still yelling, but I ignored her. I couldn't go downstairs yet, not while Grandma was still in the house. She'd try to make me go outside and talk to the reporters, and it would be harder to say no to her. Gran wasn't in a tree.

Since I couldn't go back into my room and get my CD player, not until Mom stopped yelling for me, and I couldn't go downstairs while Grandma was in the kitchen, I walked down the hall into Mom's room. Maybe I'd watch TV. Not the news or weather channel, but some channel that wouldn't show pictures of my family. The space channel would be safe. Mom's protest hadn't made it to outer space. Yet.

I lay on Mom's bed and clicked on the TV. I found a cartoon and settled down to some serious watching. I'd had enough of the tree business. I wasn't going to think about it anymore. I wasn't going to worry about Mom anymore. I wasn't even going to sigh anymore.

If Mom wanted to act that way, then let her. I didn't care. I didn't care if she went to jail. I really really didn't care.

I concentrated, or tried to, on the cartoon. It wasn't easy. I had to keep turning the volume up. Finally I realized I couldn't hear the TV because of the noise that was coming from outside.

The noise came from the front of the house, not from around the side by the maple tree where the bikers and the Grannies were singing and yelling. I went to the window and peered outside.

There was the police car, still in the middle of the road, lights flashing. But now the police car was in the center of a traffic jam.

Cars were stopped in front of it and behind it. There was an unmoving line of cars the whole length of the block. Horns honked.

People stood in the road and on the sidewalk, squeezed in between the cars and the motorbikes like jam in a sandwich.

I opened the window. The honking was louder, but now I could hear what people were saying.

"It may be a police car, but it doesn't have any right to block traffic."

"Julia will be late for her soccer game. Can't you back up so I can get out?"

"Back up to where? There's another car right on my tail. You blind or something?"

"What's going on, does anyone know?"

"It's Dian again."

"That figures."

"That tree adds character to the neighborhood. It shouldn't be cut down."

"Character, smaracter. It's on Harold's property and he has a right to take it down if he wants to. You tree huggers make me sick."

"You rednecks are so ignorant."

I recognized most of the neighbors on our block. Some were standing in front of Mr. Wilson's house; others were in front of our house. Those two groups were the ones doing most of the shouting at each other. It seemed as if everyone had taken a side.

One man had climbed onto the hood of his car and was yelling, "Move it, move it. I've got things to do."

The voices got louder—and angrier—as I listened.

"That woman's insane."

"Harold's a disgrace to the neighborhood, bringing all those bikers here."

In the distance I could hear sirens. The police backup was arriving. Because I was looking out the window, high above the crowd, I saw them first. Not more policemen. Two ordinary men wearing white coveralls were pushing a wheelbarrow toward the crowd.

As they made their way along the sidewalk, people stopped shouting and horns stopped honking. Everyone just watched. The man standing on his car came down and joined the people in front of our house. Others moved aside, clearing a path for the wheelbarrow to pass through.

No one said anything.

By the time the two men reached Mr. Wilson's house, there was not a sound from the crowded street except the squeak of the wheelbarrow's wheel.

I clearly heard one of the men say, "This is the place. I didn't know there would be so many people here."

"Doesn't matter," said the other man. "We've got a job to do."

The first man reached into the wheelbarrow and lifted something out.

His back was to me, so I couldn't see exactly what it was. He put it on the sidewalk.

"Hope she starts," he said. "Had a bit of trouble yesterday." He bent over and yanked on something a few times. Then a chain saw roared.

From Mr. Wilson's yard the bikers cheered.

They began to chant, "Take this tree out, take this tree out, take this tree out."

Harold Wilson appeared in his front yard, and the two men followed him around the side of the house to the maple tree.

The tree my mother was chained to was about to be cut down, mother and all.

Chapter Twelve

People with red hair are supposed to have bad tempers. They're supposed to get mad easily, scream a lot, have tantrums and throw things. At least that's what redheaded people in books do.

Although I have red hair, I have always thought of myself as a very patient person. I don't scream—except when someone throws a dead worm at me, or I get splashed unexpectedly at the pool.

I don't fight with my friends or my teachers. Or my mom. At least not much. I've never thrown anything—except a softball—at my friends.

But all of a sudden I could feel my face turning as red as my hair, could feel my cheeks getting hot, could feel an angry scream building inside. My fingers itched to pick something up and throw it, hard.

I was about to have a tantrum.

Everyone else was throwing tantrums. Why shouldn't I? And the people having tantrums were grown-ups. They were supposed to behave like adults. But what were they doing?

I looked out Mom's window again. The two groups of people, those in front of Mr. Wilson's house and those in front of our house, were shouting at each other.

"Tree hugger."

"Redneck."

"She's fighting for a good cause."

"He has a right to cut down *his* tree."

I went to my room, opened my window and looked out.

Mom didn't see me. She was sitting on her favorite branch, staring down at the man with the chain saw. "Don't you dare touch a leaf of this tree," she was shouting. "Or you'll be sorry."

The man in coveralls started the chain saw. "Can't hear you, lady. My saw is too loud."

Mr. Wilson held an official looking piece of paper in his hand and he waved it at Mom. "This has gone far enough, Dian. I've got a permit to remove this tree. Come down or you'll be sorry."

"I'll never come down. Never. You can't make me."

"Then we'll start cutting with you sitting on that branch," he shouted.

"You wouldn't!" Mom said.

The man with the chain saw shrugged. "Last week I took out a tree with birds in it," he said. "The mother robin wouldn't leave her nest, so down she came, nest and babies too. I guess cutting this tree with you sitting in it won't be hard." He stepped closer to the tree trunk and made the chain saw roar again.

"Sir, you can't do that. She might get hurt. We'll call the fire department. They'll get her down," said one of the policemen. He was the only adult who sounded polite, but he also sounded nervous.

He looked up at Mom. "Ma'am, this gentleman has asked you to vacate his property. Please leave the tree at once."

"Crazy lady, crazy lady, crazy lady," chanted the bikers. One of them actually made a face at Mom, sticking his tongue out. "Nutzoid," he said. "You're from nut city."

"Says who?" screamed a sweet little old lady. Make that a not-so-sweet-right-now little old lady: my grandma. "You touch a hair on my daughter's head and I'll pull that leather vest right off your hairy chest and scratch your tattoos off with my bare fingernails!"

"Right! Let's rip those tattoos off," shouted one of the Grannies, and they began to sing a new song. It sounded a lot like the bikers song only you could recognize the tune of "Twinkle, Twinkle, Little Star."

"Bikers, bikers, stand aside, stupid bikers just go ride."

"Who you calling stupid?" asked Duke. "Watch your mouths, you old bags."

"Old bags, old bags, stand aside; old bags, old bags stand aside," chanted a biker, and then they all began saying it.

The narrow space between our house and Mr. Wilson's fence was packed with people—Grannies, reporters, two policemen and a few neighbors. Someone had brought a dog. The poor animal was squished in the middle of the crowd, human legs all around him like bars of a jail cell. He looked as if he wanted to get out of there as soon as possible. I knew exactly how he felt.

There was more room on Mr. Wilson's side of the fence. But his yard, too, was crammed with people.

The bikers took up most of the space, mainly because they were bigger than anyone else. They hung over the fence, shouting at the Grannies. There were more reporters in Mr. Wilson's yard than there were in ours. They had a better view of Mom from there because they weren't right underneath the branch she was sitting on. There were also two policemen in his yard—the police backup must have arrived—and some neighbors, as well as the men with the chain saw.

The reporters pointed cameras over the bikers' shoulders, shouting at Mom to look their way. A microphone on a long stick waved in the branches and reporters held smaller microphones up as high as they could.

"Give us a sound bite, Dian," one of them said. "Come on, say something that will sound good on the news. Hurry. I've got a deadline."

I could hear more sirens wailing. Probably it was the firefighters, coming to haul Mom out of the tree. How would they do that? Tie her up? Throw her over their shoulders and carry her down a ladder the way they do in movies?

Mom wouldn't like that. She'd scream and kick and shout. Maybe she'd wriggle so much she'd fall and hurt herself and be in hospital for months. Then what would happen to me? I'd have to go and live with Gran at her place where they don't like kids visiting, much less actually moving in.

Or go to Ottawa and stay with my dad and the twins.

"Old bags."

"Stupid bikers."

"Louts."

"Crazy woman."

"Tree murderer."

"Hey, our time's valuable. We've got other trees to deal with this morning. Let's get on with it or we're leaving."

I looked down at the dog. He had backed up against the fence, and he still looked as if he wanted to get out of there as soon as he could. But I no longer wanted to leave. I wanted to shout, to scream, to yell, make them all listen to me. I had something I needed to say, and I was going to say it.

I was going to yell too, just like the grown-ups were doing. It was my turn.

Reaching under my bed, I yanked out the board. I shoved it out the window and hooked it onto a branch. Then I climbed out and sat on it.

"Hey!" I shouted. "Up here."

At first, no one saw me. Then, "Hi, Daffy, welcome to the madhouse," someone called.

I waved at Peter, and the cameras swung my way.

"Her daughter's up there with her. Smile, Callie."

I didn't feel like smiling, so I scowled. Mom smiled. The bikers glared. The Grannies sang. The reporters clicked cameras and shouted questions.

I said something. No one heard me over the noise.

I said it again, louder. Again, no one heard me.

So I stood up on the board and took a few steps closer to Mom and the tree house. "Listen to me," I shouted. "Listen to..."

The board began to slip.

Chapter Thirteen

"Callie, be careful!" called Mom, and she lunged sideways along the branch, reaching out for me.

That was not a smart thing to do. The hooks on the board were around the same branch Mom was sitting on. As she moved toward me, the branch bent under her weight. The hooks slipped farther down the branch and the board twisted.

I knew I was going to fall, so I grabbed for the branch above me. I missed.

"Callie!" screamed Mom.

I grabbed for another branch and caught it. But I didn't have a firm grip. I dangled from that branch for what seemed like a long time but was probably only a few seconds. Then my fingers slipped and I fell.

Someone said "oomph" very loudly.

"Glad you could drop in, Daffy," said Peter breathlessly. "Now, if you could get off me, both of us could stand up. Are you all right?"

"Yes. Thank you, Uncle...Peter." I stood up, slowly. "Are you hurt?"

"I don't know yet," he said. I looked down at him. He lay on the ground, his glasses sideways on his face, his hair even more wispy. "Give me a minute to catch my breath."

One of the policemen on our side of the fence pushed through the Grannies' bobbing hats and the reporters' cameras and knelt beside him. "Sir, can you hear me? How many fingers am I holding up? What day is it? Who is our prime minister?"

Peter pushed the policeman aside and slowly stood up. "I didn't know having falling kids land on you meant you had to take a current affairs test. Ouch!" He rubbed his shoulder.

"Are you hurt, sir?" asked the policeman again.

"No. But Callie packs quite a punch. Especially with her feet, which I think landed on my shoulders."

"You saved that kid from serious injury," said a reporter, shoving a microphone in Peter's face. "How does it feel to be a hero?"

"Hero? Me?" asked Peter.

It had been quiet around the tree, or I think it had—I'd been too busy falling to notice—but suddenly it seemed everyone was shouting again. At me.

"What was it like to narrowly escape death?" a reporter asked me.

"Did your whole life flash before your eyes?" said another.

The reporters were crazy. I wouldn't have fallen far enough to seriously hurt myself, even if I hadn't landed on Peter.

"Could you look frightened?" asked a photographer.

"Callie, are you all right?" called Mom, leaning over so far she was in danger of falling out of the tree herself.

Several of the Grannies were crying. Two of the bikers had climbed over the fence and were hovering around Peter. One of them patted him on the shoulder, and I heard another "ouch." The reporters were all talking at once, and the cameras whirred and clicked.

The biker with the big stomach climbed over the fence, more slowly than the other two. "Hey, kid, you okay?" he asked me.

"Yes," I said. "But I need help, Duke. Lift me up so people can see me."

"Huh?"

"Just do it. Please." I wasn't angry anymore, but there was something I wanted to say. I needed to be up high so everyone could see me and hear me, but I didn't feel like climbing into the tree again.

Duke grabbed me around the waist and lifted me up to his shoulders. "Listen to me," I called.

No one paid any attention.

"Hey!" roared Duke. "You heard the little lady. Shut up and listen."

It took a few seconds, but finally everyone was looking at me. "As I was trying to tell you before I fell out of the tree," I said, "*we* have a garage."

"She doesn't know what she's saying," said my gran. "She must have a head injury. We need to take her to the hospital."

"We don't have a car," I said.

"We'll call an ambulance," said Mom. "Don't worry, we'll get you there. Try to stay calm, you're delirious."

"I'm *not* delirious!" I shouted. "Just be quiet and listen to me. You're acting like kindergarten kids. Shouting. Calling each other names. You should be ashamed of yourselves."

It was suddenly quiet. Very quiet.

I took a deep breath. "It's so easy to solve this problem, if you'd all stop shouting and think about it. Mom has a garage. She doesn't have a car. If she lets Mr. Wilson use her garage for his motorcycle, he won't have to cut down the tree."

It stayed silent for what seemed like a long time. Then Mr. Wilson said, "The garage roof probably leaks."

"It does not," answered Mom. "But I have things stored in there."

"Mom, there's nothing in there except your old potter's wheel and a lot of junk you're always saying you're going to get rid of. We keep our bikes in the basement. We don't need the garage. Why don't we let Mr. Wilson use it?"

"But...," said Mom.

"But...," said Harold Wilson.

"Huh?" said Duke.

"Mr. Wilson," I said, "if you want to use our garage instead of building a new one, I'm sure Mom will agree. Right, Mom?"

"But...," said my mother again.

"But what a wonderful solution," said my grandmother, beaming. "That girl has her grandfather's good common sense."

"Thanks, Gran. Why don't we all take a look at our garage?"

"Sure, little lady, let's see it," said Duke, lowering me to the ground.

We all went to look: reporters, bikers, Grannies, policemen, Josie, me, the other kids and even the dog. Mom stayed up the tree, just in case.

"This place is full," said Gran as we peered in the door. "There's no room for Harold's bike."

"So let's have a garage sale," I said.

"But we have to advertise to get people to come," said Gran.

"No we don't. There are enough people here right now. Let's have an instant garage sale."

Gran went back to the tree and talked to Mom. Then Mom undid the lock, took off the chain around her ankle and climbed down the tree. Everyone cheered.

Mom took a look in the garage, then announced, "Callie's right. I don't need to keep any of this stuff. All right, Harold, it's a deal."

Mr. Wilson and the bikers had been checking out the garage too. "It's big enough," he said. "If you're sure it doesn't leak, Dian, then okay, I agree. I get to use your garage and the tree stays."

They shook hands, and there was more cheering while cameras went into double time, flashing and clicking.

Then Mom announced, "Make your offers, people. Everything must be sold."

Everything did sell, and it didn't take long.

A CBC reporter bought Mom's old potter's wheel, the weather channel photographer took the planters we don't use anymore and the bikers paid for three boxes of old towels and sheets. They said they were going to turn them into rags to clean their bikes.

The Grannies found brooms and scrub brushes and went to work. In less than an hour the garage was empty and cleaner than it had been in years.

Peter ordered pizza, while the bikers took up a collection. The reporters and Grannies chipped in. There was enough money to buy pizza and pop for everyone.

Josie wouldn't let us use the money she had collected. She and the other kids decided to give it to the food bank.

Everyone ate, even the policemen and the dog. While they were eating, the policemen had a meeting. They decided that Mom hadn't been holding a real protest, the kind that needed a permit. So she hadn't been breaking the law and they didn't need to arrest her or make her pay a fine. Everyone talked, laughed a lot and shook hands. Then they all went away.

Except Mom and me. And Peter Dawl. Mom wouldn't let him leave.

"There's an old Chinese belief," she told him, "that if you save a person's life, you are responsible for that person for the rest of *your* life. You can start being responsible right now, Peter. Callie's room is a mess. I've been staring at it through her window for two days. Please get her to clean it up."

"I don't think…," began Peter.

"Mom!" I said at the same time.

"Well, it was worth a try," said Mom. "But I guess nagging is a mother's job. You'll stay for supper, won't you, Peter? Since you saved Callie's life, I feel as if you are a member of the family."

I sighed. Again. "Just call him Uncle Ken," I said. "And he didn't save my life. I didn't fall that far."

"Far enough to break a few bones if he hadn't caught you," said Mom.

"Actually, I didn't catch…"

But Mom went right on talking. "Seriously, Peter—Ken—we are very grateful to you. If there's anything I can do…"

There was.

Before he left that night, Peter got his exclusive—an interview not just with Mom but also with Mr. Wilson. He wanted to do an interview with me too, but I said no way. This whole tree thing was Mom's idea. I didn't want anyone to read about me in the paper and think I'd had anything to do with it. I was proud that I had solved the problem when all the grown-ups couldn't, but not proud enough to want my picture taken again.

Peter asked Mom and Mr. Wilson lots of questions. He made them climb up the tree and took pictures of them sitting in front of the tree house. Then he came back inside, pulled out his laptop and began writing. I made popcorn and waited for dinner.

An hour later I was starving and thinking about using the money from the